WELCOME!

We are incredibly excited to have you joining us for this Start to DJ Program! This is the beginning of something that will enhance your relationship with music, increase your confidence and will be a fun and enjoyable journey!

I never thought that DJing would take me around the world, working with artists that I admire and finding community and a home with like-minded people that love music and technology the same way I do!

I am honored to be your Coach and work alongside your Campus Coach to help you through the next 8 Sessions, on your road to creating your first mix, or best mix yet. Let's jump in!

GET STARTED

- Go through the Session with your Campus Coach and Team
- Fill out the workbook as you go
- Take your workbook with you to review
- Access your DJ software on the go at home
- Go deeper with the First 50 DJ Techniques Book

Helpful Hints throughout the workbook:

PRO TIP

COACH SAYS:

FIRST 50 CONCEPTS: #3, #20, #40

SESSION 1:

Start TO DJ

My DJ Name is:

Name of Teammate or Coach:

FIRST 50 CONCEPTS: #1, #2, #25, #44

BPM stands for: B_______ P_____ M__________

Why is BPM important for DJs?

(Describe the best way you possibly can)

Where is BPM found on the left deck? Circle it

What is another word to describe BPM?

HINT: Starts with a "T" and is 5 letters

What is the button that I push to get the tempo of both songs to be the same?

a. Beat Sync
b. Tempo Reset
c. Hot Cue
d. Play

COACH SAYS:

Trust the Process! We will get there together by taking it one step at a time!

Which step does NOT belong?

(Cross it out)

Hit Play on the 1st song

Beat Sync

Hit Play on the 2nd song

Use the Echo FX

Use the Crossfader or Volume Faders

volume
bpm
crossfader
disc jockey
sync
music
tempo

BONUS:
StartToDJ

```
B Y M X M E M F A V A Z O U P K A V T Y
I A D H M R U K B B G Z G A A M V S Y Q
I R W K P L S Y P N G F C S F O W I Z Q
F S Q G V T I O U Z M Q C E E T R T A M
R S B D C G C Y T E M P O E O D E V D E
R O C H S V D O L Z G Z R R F J O W N Z
O J Z C E R O X O V Q R S Q I E P H S U
J Q J X C R O S S F A D E R K C F Q Y R
A X T N Q X W H C Y H V Y D A G L C N K
W F J U U K N R B P M J G F E F J C C D
V N K I H R D W J W X Y N Q Q H U X Z I
O G S L U K M X K M W A E Q S U A B R S
L G N T A A L T Y D Z Y S T U O V G W C
U P A K R G T Z M U Z M D A M B U X F J
M V H D D W H Z A B Y U T J D N K A U O
E S S V S W N W Y M D D H L S Z W C V C
X Q W T Z Y R C F Y Z Y I J R T E N Q K
H H C S U D B B V K M X P S I S P W C E
L U W G O G B R V Q S T A R T T O D J Y
T S T X D F X L B U U H R A G Y P F G Q
```

DDJ-FLX4

CIRCLE the following for the LEFT deck:

Tempo Fader	Play Button
Beat Sync Button	Channel Fader

Pioneer DJ

Now, CIRCLE the following for the RIGHT deck:

Tempo Fader

Beat Sync Button

Play Button

Channel Fader

SESSION 2:

Start TO DJ

My DJ Name is:

Name two teammates:

FIRST 50 CONCEPTS: #3, #20, #40

What is a beat?

A H____________________

What is another word to describe BPM?

a. Sync
b. Tempo
c. Speed
d. Time

What does a red hot cue represent?

a. 4 Bars
b. 4 Beats
c. 8 Beats
d. 8 Bars

Why shouldn't you mix vocals over vocals?

If my song is at 100 BPM, based on our "rule of thumb" fill in the two maximum and minimum numbers

+/- ☐

☐ ⟵ **100** ⟶ ☐

If a song I'm mixing out of is 90 BPM, I can mix a track thats 108 BPM.

TRUE **FALSE**

What is the button that I push to get the tempo of both songs to be the same?

- ○ Beat Sync
- ○ Tempo Reset
- ○ Hot Cue
- ○ Play

What does EDM stand for?

	EDM
INTRO	
VERSE	BUILD
PRE-CHORUS	
CHORUS	DROP
BRIDGE	BREAKDOWN
OUTRO	OTHER SECTIONS?

DDJ-FLX4

CIRCLE the following for the LEFT deck:

First Hot Cue
Beat Sync Button
Jogwheel
Channel Fader

COACH SAYS:

Focus on the similarities instead of the differences with dj equipment. You might not have this exact same controller, but they all work similarly! Find these controls on your DJ rig (or even inside of the software).

Now, CIRCLE the following for the RIGHT deck:

First Hot Cue

Beat Sync Button

Jogwheel

Channel Fader

SESSION 3:

What is a bar?

Circle all that apply. There might be more than one answer!

a. 4 Beats
b. 8 Beats
c. 4 Headnods

FIRST 50 CONCEPTS: #3, #19, #20

Fill in the missing numbers:

4 BARS	**LOOP**
___ BARS	**JUMP TO**
12 BARS	
___ BARS	

Where do we set the hot cue in relation to the section?

a. The beginning of the section (intro)

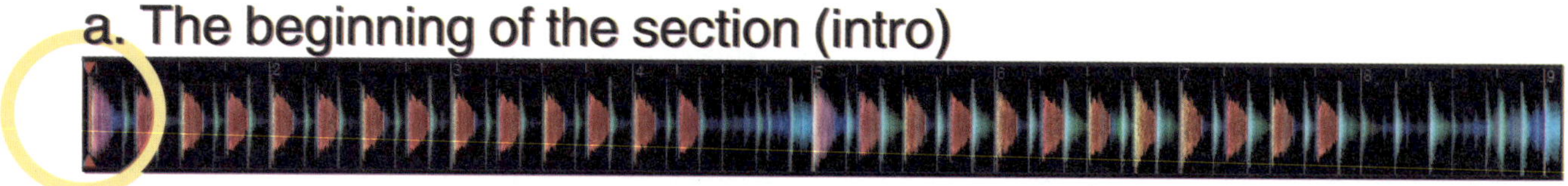

b. The end of the section (intro)

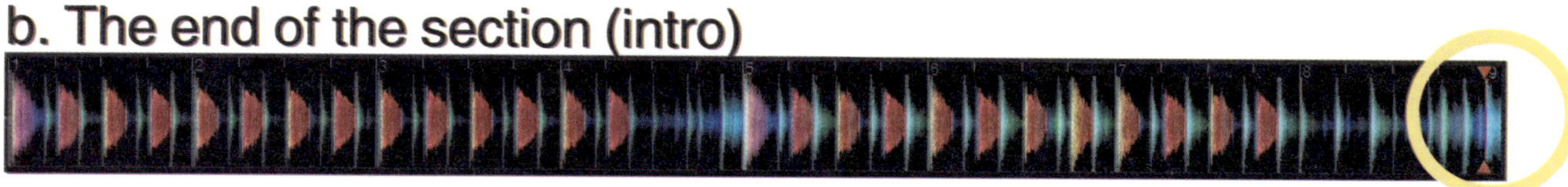

If my song is at 122 BPM, based on our "rule of thumb" fill in the two maximum and minimum numbers

+/- ☐

☐ ⟵ 122 ⟶ ☐

All songs of a particular genre of music have the SAME structure.

TRUE **FALSE**

How many hot cues can I create per track?

a. 4
b. 6
c. 8
d. 16

Name 3 of your favorite songs right now?
How can you find out the BPM of these songs?

	SONG NAME	BPM
1.		
2.		
3.		

SETTING HOT CUES

STEP 1: Click on this icon to open more options

STEP 2: Click on this icon to get to hot cues

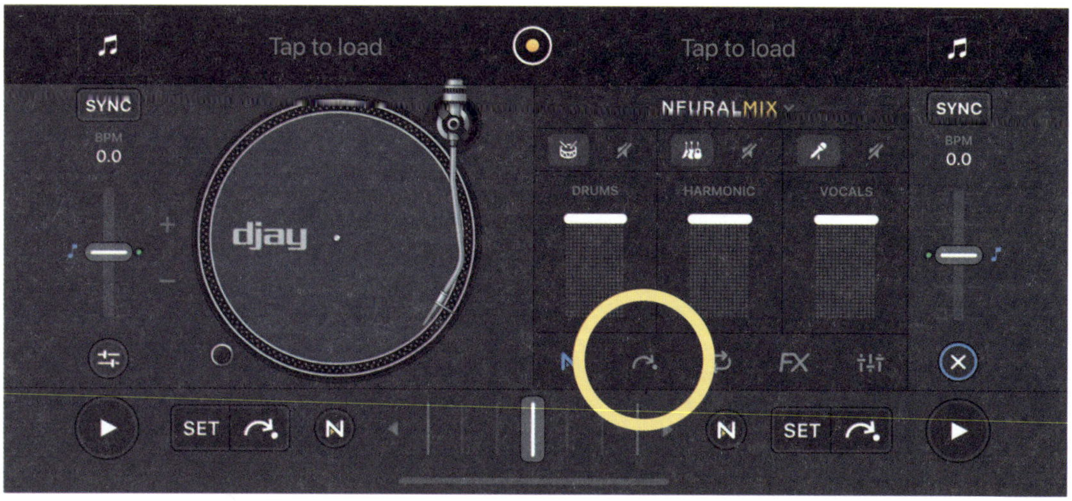

STEP 3: Click on the "+" to set your hot cue

STEP 4: Click on the pencil icon to edit the color and type a note

STEP 5: Follow the map when you play!

Remember, all you have to do is line up the colors when you are playing and the phrasing should be correct if you got the map right!

You can try this with our demo tracks. If you line up the beginning of the intro (red) with the beginning of the chorus (red), they should mix well together!

COACH SAYS:

Setting Hot Cues will help you break your songs down and will ultimately give you more confidence and freedom when mixing live! It takes some time and effort, but it's no different from learning how to play songs on the piano or guitar.
Put in the time and it'll pay off!
This is **easily** the most important concept to learn as a DJ!

SESSION 4:

Start TO DJ

FIRST 50 CONCEPTS:
#4, #32, #40

Match the following lengths:

a. 4 Beats	a. 1 Bar
b. 8 Beats	b. 3 Bars
c. 12 Headnods	c. 1/2 Phrase
d. 8 Bars	d. 16 Bars
e. 4 Phrases	e. 2 Phrases

Anatomy of the Mix:

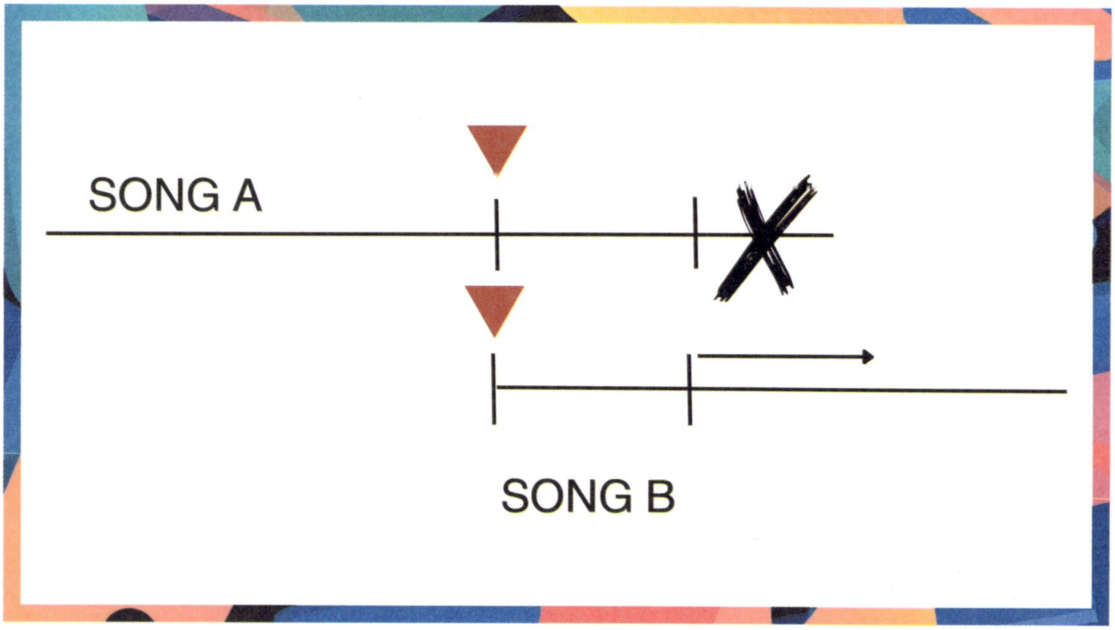

Answer the following:

How long is the intro of Song B? _____ Bars

How long is the chorus of Song A? _____ Bars

What two parts of these two songs would be playing together?

Fill in the blanks:

(yellow)	__ **BARS**	(green)	**LOOP**
(brown)	__ **BARS**	(light blue)	**JUMP TO**
(dark blue)	__ **BARS**		
(pink)	__ **BARS**		

If I use the EQ, I don't need to use the volume faders

TRUE **FALSE**

If I were to tell you to make a new sandwich out of these two, would you just stack them on top of each other?

COACH SAYS:

We don't believe "Practice Makes Perfect".
We believe that "Proper Practice Makes Progress". Try to throw the idea of "perfect" out the window and I know if you're like me, that might be a challenge. We want to focus on making progress - one step at a time. Just try to find one thing that you can be 1% better at today!

SMOOTHING OUT THE MIX

STEP 1: Make sure the tracks are properly mapped out and have hot cues on them

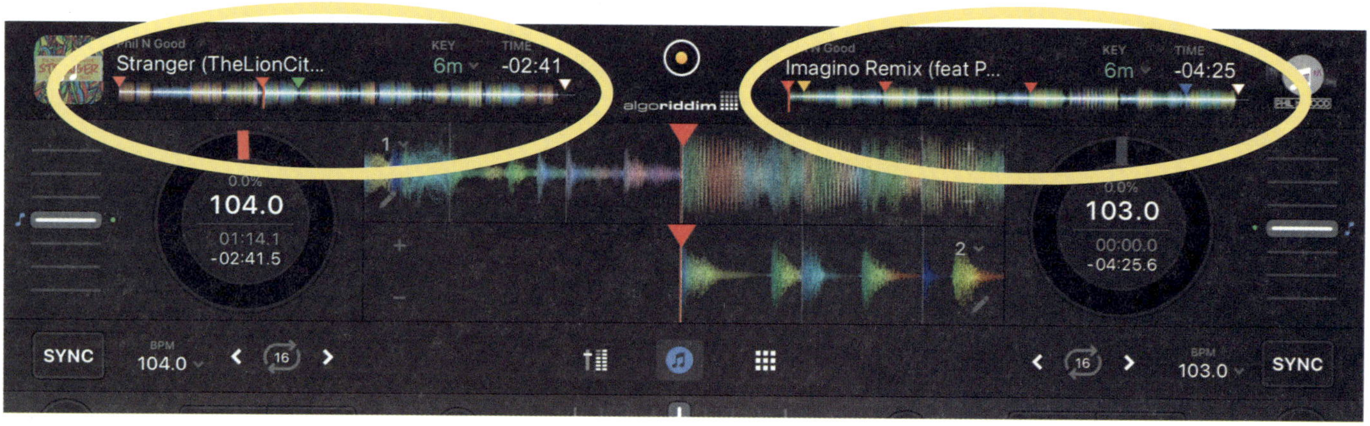

STEP 2: Get ready to bring in the second song as the first chorus is approaching

STEP 3: Beat sync the tracks and hit play on the second track on time, lining up Red and Red Hot Cues

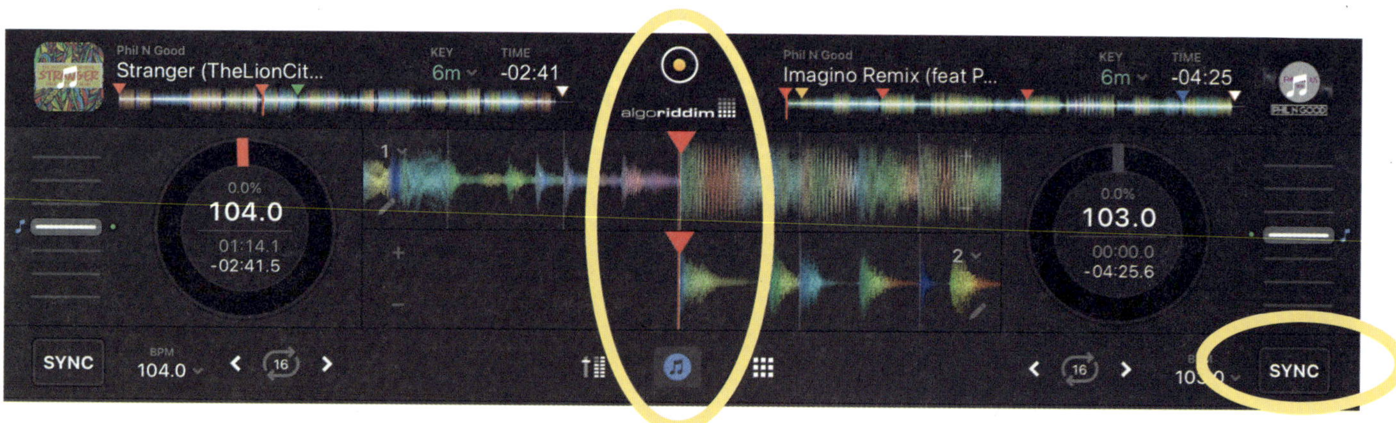

STEP 4: Bring the volume up on the right deck

STEP 5: Use the EQ of the right and left deck to smooth out the mix by taking out the low end of the left deck.

STEP 6: Use your best judgement to feel out what else you should take out from the EQ as the songs are mixing

OLD SCHOOL CLOCK

The default position for "unity" or where the EQ knobs should be in order to play the song as it was originally supposed to sound would be 12 o'clock (green).

You should really try to avoid going past 3 o'clock for the most part on the EQ to prevent distortion (yellow)

The LED meters will also show you whether or not you are "redlining" or pushing the EQ and sound too far on each channel.

SESSION 5:

What does HPF stand for?

H_______ P________ F______________

What does LPF stand for?

L_______ P________ F______________

What would you mostly hear if you had the HPF turned up?

a. Mostly mid frequencies
b. Mostly high frequencies
c. Mostly low frequencies
d. More volume

What's wrong with this picture?

Try to remember what we talked about last session with EQ!

PRO TIP

"Redlining is not headlining"

There are memes floating around that say, "If you're not redlining, you're not headlining" and it's just plain wrong!

This refers to the main DJ (headliner) who would be the star of the night. No matter if you're a headliner or not, learn to control the sound, minimize the distortion and watch your levels.

Not every song has an 8 bar chorus. In this example, Song A and B have different size intros and chorus:

Anatomy of the Mix:

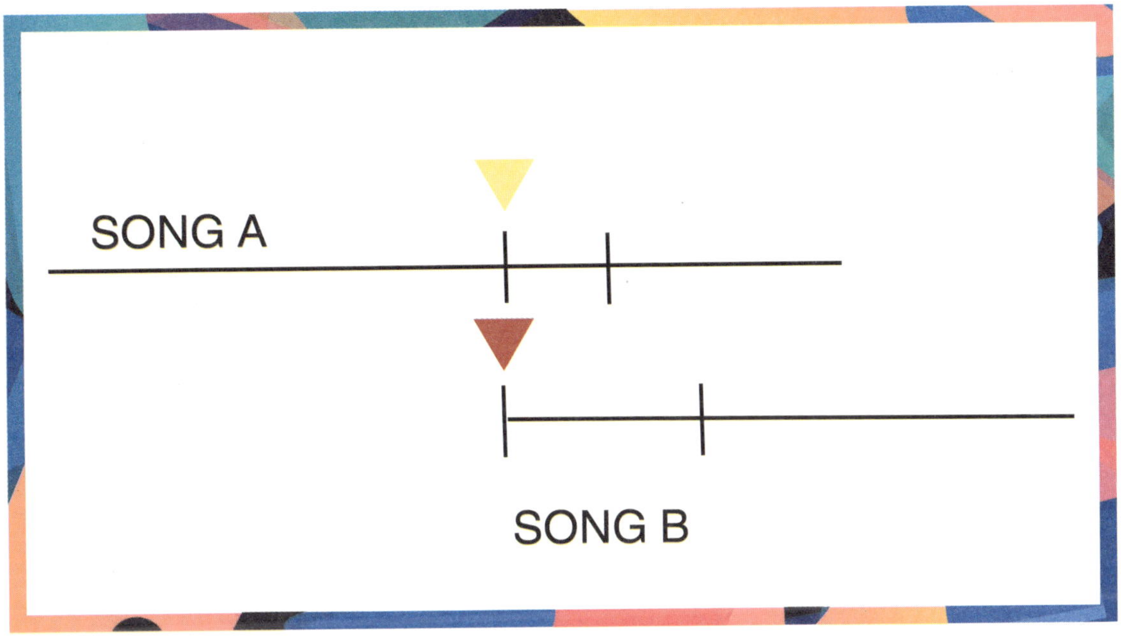

What would be wrong about this image?

How long is the intro of Song B? _____ Bars

How long is the chorus of Song A? _____ Bars

How can I fix this?

There's more than one answer to get this back on track!

FILTER FX

Use the Filter to bend frequencies when mixing tracks or to add tension. 12 o'clock will turn the Filter off.

DIFFERENT CFX

There are other options for "Color FX" that can be controlled with this knob. This will be changed inside of your software of choice.

Options for CFX inside of rekordbox

COACH SAYS:

Moderation is key!

Sometimes adding too much FX can actually take away from the mix. It's like when you're cooking and you add too many spices to your dish. There's no amount of salt you can add to an undercooked chicken that will save it. Same with a poorly phrased mix and FX.

BEAT FX

There are two different categories of Beat FX.

RHYTHM FX	NON-RHYTHM FX
Delay	Reverb
Echo	Pan
Spiral	Filter
Reverse Delay	Flanger
MT Delay	Phaser
Up Echo	Robot
Down Echo	Pitch
Trans	Enigma Jet
Gate	Mobius Saw
Roll	Mobius Tri
Slip Roll	LFO Filter
Reverse Roll	Distortion
Low Cut Echo	LPF
Echo Out	HPF

If using Rhythm FX, the "Beat" function is critical!

TRY THIS!

Use the Delay as a 1/2 or 1/4 beat while the track is playing. Move the level/depth knob as the Delay is on and try and stay on beat. What do you hear?

SESSION 6:

FIRST 50 CONCEPTS: #34, #35

When I see "1" in the Loop section, what is that length in terms of?

a. Bars
b. Beats
c. Seconds
d. Phrases

What does the "Bounce" feature do inside of the Loop menu?

Mark all that are true!

a. Loops the section while the track is still playing underneath
b. Loops when you are holding the pad down
c. Releases to where the track would have been if you didn't hit Bounce when you let go of the pad

KOOL HERC - LIVE LOOPING!

- 1973
- Sedwick + Cedar Ave, Bronx, New York
- Clive Campbell aka Kool DJ Herc
- Funk, Disco Vinyl Records
- Two turntables and a pre-amp mixer
- GOAL: Keep the kids dancing
- **IMPACT: PRICELESS**

Kool Herc photo by MinusBaby at English Wikipedia, licensed under Creative Commons Attribution-Share Alike 3.0 International

DJs like Kool Herc discovered that the kids would only dance during the bridge, or break of the disco songs. That was great, but was also a problem. The break was just that, a short break from the "cheesy" singing of the song that was "mom and dad's music".

AHA!

While the break is playing, and kids are dancing, I get a 2nd copy of the same song, cue it up to the beginning of the break, and then restart it on time before the first break ends?!

IT WORKED!

The kids kept dancing and even started doing moves they saw James Brown doing on TV, but putting their own spin to it. Herc called these break boys and break girls and the style of dance, break dancing since, well, they were dancing during the break.

LOOP ROLL JUST DRUMS

STEP 1: Click on this icon to open more options

STEP 2: Click on this icon to get to hot cues

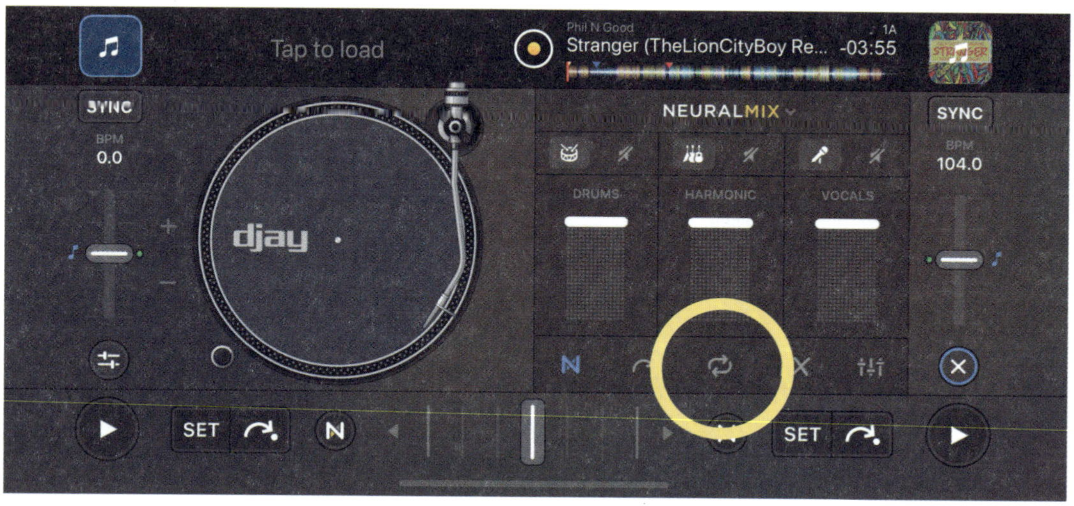

STEP 3: Click on "Bounce"

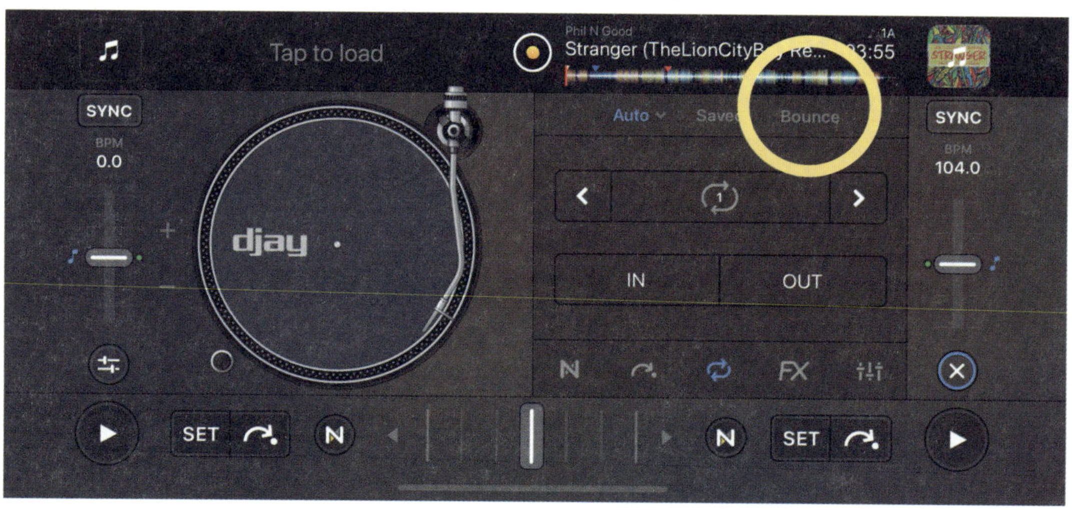

STEP 4: Click on this icon to split the song to its drum stem

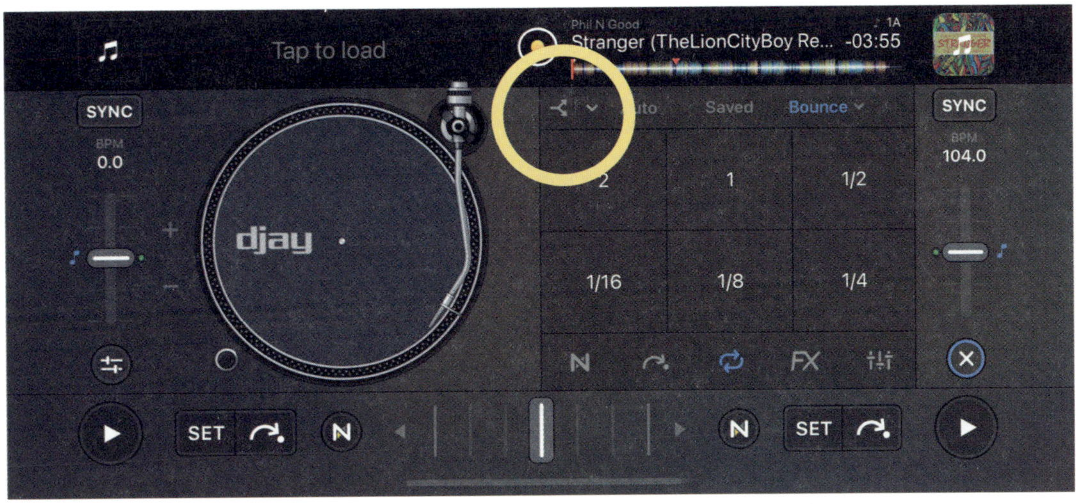

STEP 5: I like using the 1/2 or 1/4

COACH SAYS:

Learning about the history of this culture is incredibly facinating. Did you know that Kool Herc doesn't have a Grammy or isn't in the Rock and Roll Hall of Fame?! This lesson may sound a lot about "Hip Hop History" (which it is), but it's also MUCH broader! 99% of the music today is produced with loops. Think about that! Imagine if Kool Herc was paid a penny for each song that was made with a loop?!

I encourage you to learn more about the history of things you are interested in and to share this story with others!

SESSION 7:

Start TO DJ

What are headphones for?

Mark all that are true!

a. To "look like a DJ"

b. To listen to the next song you are getting ready to play

c. To make sure the beats are lined up

d. To make sure the songs sound good together

FIRST 50 CONCEPTS: #23, #49

Could I use these to DJ with?

Circle your answer:

YES **NO**

BASIC SCRATCHING!

Scratching is incredibly fun and can add a lot of flavor to your performance. It can also demonstrate a level of confidence and control and will even help you with your mixing!

Which one is back at the beginning of the sample?

A

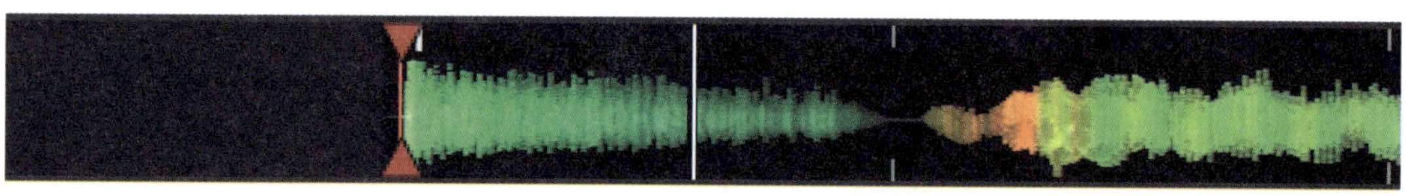

B

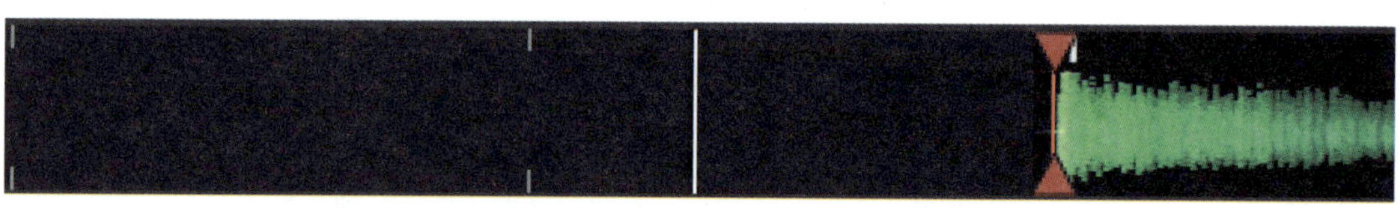

C

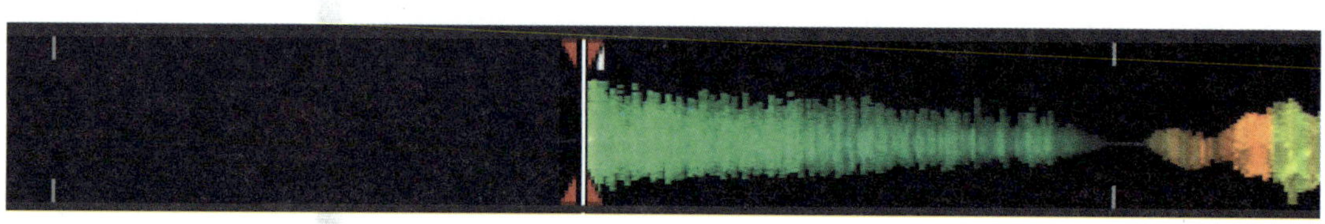

There are two parts of the jogwheel

TOP: Used for scratching, rewinding and fastforwarding the track, backspins

SIDE: Used for speeding up and slowing down the track temporarily

How many sounds are in one bar of 1/8 notes?

a. 8 b. 16 c. 4

PRO TIP:

Make sure to move your body to the music when you scratch and try not to overthink it!

FINDING THE SAMPLER

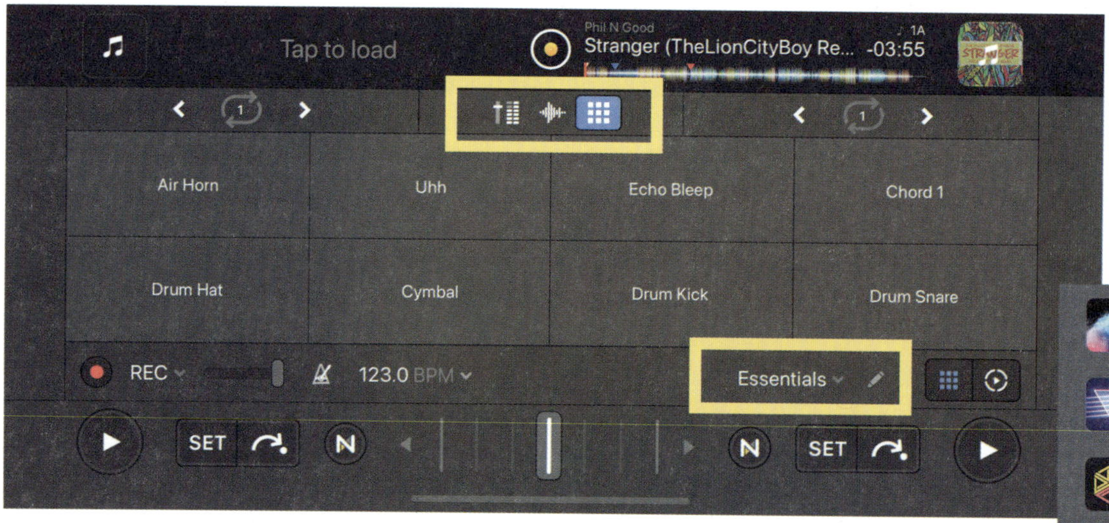

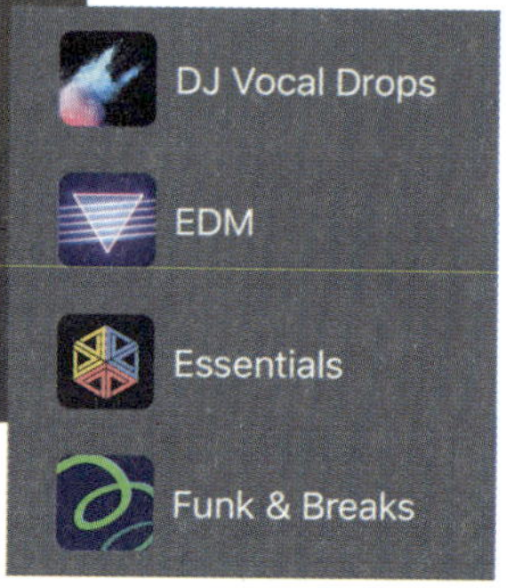

Can you customize your own pack?

YES NO

SESSION 8:

Start TO DJ

Today is the day!
Time to put it all together!
Make sure to take it step-by-step
and enjoy it!

MILESTONE 1!
YOUR 6 SONG MIX

DJ ____________________ Set List

	Song Name	BPM
1.		
2.		
3.		
4.		
5.		
6.		

Remember to pay attention to the BPMs and try and group like-BPM songs together and TRUST your maps!

COACH SAYS:

Progression over Perfection!
Remember to have fun with this set and that this is the "before" picture. This is just where you are at right now and look at you - 8 Sessions ago you couldn't do ANY of this and now here you are! I'm really proud of your progress and this took me **years** to get to this point you're at!

FEEDBACK

Honest feedback from our peers is how we grow! Have a friend or coach fill this out for you as you perform your set.

The more specific you are, the better! Telling someone "your mix was great" is not helpful. What was great about it? What could be improved upon?

THINGS I DID WELL:

1.

2.

SOMETHING I CAN IMPROVE ON:

1.

WHAT'S NEXT?

Ask your Campus Coach about Level 2 or reach out to our staff@thedjcoach.com

CERTIFICATE OF RECOGNITION

This is hereby awarded to

in recognition of their excellent participation with the
Start to DJ Program - Level 1

Campus Coach

HAPA BRANDON PERDUE
Head Coach, TheDJCoach.com